WILLPOWER

21 DAY CHALLENGE TO PUSH THROUGH ANYTHING, RESIST TEMPTATION AND ACHIEVE YOUR GOALS - HOW TO KEEP GOING WHEN YOU WANT TO GIVE UP

I0477706

"WILLPOWER IS TRYING VERY HARD NOT TO DO SOMETHING YOU WANT TO DO VERY MUCH." - JOHN ORTBERG

Legal & Disclaimer

The information contained in this book is not designed to replace or take the place of any form of medicine or professional medical advice. The information in this book has been provided for educational and entertainment purposes only.

The information contained in this book has been compiled from sources deemed reliable, and it is accurate to the best of the Author's knowledge; however, the Author cannot guarantee its accuracy and validity and cannot be held liable for any errors or omissions. Changes are periodically made to this book. You must consult your doctor or get professional medical advice before using any of the suggested remedies, techniques, or information in this book.

TABLE OF CONTENTS

"PEOPLE DO NOT LACK STRENGTH; THEY LACK WILL." - VICTOR HUGO

INTRODUCTION

We all came across exceptional individuals with an unshakable confidence, mental strength and a burning desire to move forward despite great difficulties and challenges. No matter what stands in their way, they just maintain a forward momentum, break through the obstacles and reach their goals. Sometimes they even move beyond their perceived limitations and overcome challenges that seem insurmountable, impossible and impractical to solve. These individuals seem to have limitless mental energy and show an amazing ability to adjust and adapt in rapid changing circumstances. We term their innate psychological trait as "Willpower".

Willpower is the ability to persist in the face of adversity and bounce back from setbacks and repeated failures. It's an ability to limit temptations in order to attain long-term goals. Having willpower is about finding the inner-strength to overcome limiting beliefs and the motivation to exercise will. We all exert willpower, everyday, in one form or another. When you reach for salad when you have craving for burger, when you resist the temptation of drinking alcohol and go for a walk, when you ignore the urge to use social media instead of finishing your expense report— any time you try to do something that goes against your impulses, habits and desires, you are using some degree of willpower. Willpower separates us from animals, because through willpower, we restrain our impulses, make the right choice and do what is good for us in the long run.

A lot of research has been done on various aspects of human mind and brain. So far the researchers still haven't discovered how to permanently boost intelligence. But they have learned that we can strengthen our willpower by training it. They have also learned that we need willpower in order to enjoy a happy and successful life.

In this book, we will learn how to exercise our willpower and use it to break through life's barriers and achieve success. In this 21-day program, we will learn effective willpower strategies to set goals, smash our comfort zones and discover our potentials to attain goals. We will also learn how to bounce back from failure and move ahead when we want to give up.

"WILLPOWER IS THE KEY TO SUCCESS.
SUCCESSFUL PEOPLE STRIVE NO MATTER WHAT
THEY FEEL BY APPLYING THEIR WILL TO
OVERCOME APATHY, DOUBT OR FEAR."

- DAN MILLMAN

TRAINING YOUR WILLPOWER MUSCLE

Willpower is like mental muscle. If you exercise your muscles, they will get stronger. If you don't use them, they will get weaker. Like muscles, willpower will also tire if you use it repeatedly throughout the day. If we learn to nurture and develop our will muscle, it will help us to dig deep and keep going, even against crushing odds. The 21-day willpower challenge is a program designed to strengthen your willpower muscles through various exercises that will help you to overcome life's challenges and achieve your goals. By honing your willpower, you'll learn how to push through anything and stay determined when things get tough. It is a step-by-step program. In each step, we will discuss one key idea, and how it can be applied to your goals. The ideas and methods build on each other. So what you do in each session (each day), prepares you for the next. Therefore it is recommended not to skip any session. Let's begin:

"MY FATHER TAUGHT ME NOT TO OVERTHINK

THINGS, THAT NOTHING WILL EVER BE PERFECT,

SO JUST KEEP MOVING AND DO YOUR BEST."

-SCOTT EASTWOOD

DAY ONE

Moving Forward

When it comes to boosting your willpower, the very first thing you have to keep in mind is not to allow yourself to get stuck. Getting stuck is a common problem for many of us. Sometimes we feel that we simply can't move on with our life. We feel like we're stuck in the quicksand— the harder we try, the deeper we sink. We feel overwhelmed and don't know what to do. So what we can do to get unstuck? The best we can do is to take a different approach to address the underlying problem. On the first day of our willpower challenge, we will do something that will help us to pull ourselves out from being stuck and regain our motivation to keep moving forward. The simple thing we are going to do today will also give us a fresh start, a clean slate, an opportunity to re-invent our life. Today we will learn the art of de-cluttering.

The Art of De-cluttering

It may sound strange, but clutter in your physical environments gets in the way of the success you are reaching for. In order to de-clutter your mind and emotion, first you have to rid yourself of material clutter. De-cluttering your physical environment (which applies to the physical space you spend your time on a day-to-day basis: your home, office, even your car) will give your willpower a boost and help you to step out of your comfort zone. By taking up the willpower challenge, you are inviting a big change in your life. To welcome the big change, you not just have to prepare our mind; you also have to prepare your physical environment.

We will start with de-cluttering our home. Here are the steps you have to follow:

- Schedule the time. Give yourself 30 solid minutes. We have to start somewhere. Let's start with the most visible. You might start with a bit of rubbish or some pieces of paper lying around. Grab a trash bag and see how quickly you can fill it. Staffs may include cracked ceramic pots, water-damaged straw baskets, expired medicines, junk mails and single socks— dump all the items that no longer serve you. Gather all your lists, calendars, refrigerator message board and electronic gadgets. Sort through the information and get rid of unnecessary items. Discard the notes and lists that are no longer valid. Put papers like old bills, receipts and visiting cards in one of your business folders to sort them out later. Make a drop site on your desk, bookshelf or kitchen counter to put all the current mails, notes and receipts. Also set up separate spots for magazines/newspapers and important documents. Round up all the rubbishes and put in the trash bag.
- Next step is to de-clutter your clothing, shoes, handbags and accessories. Are there nearly as

9

many cloths on the floor and covering the furniture as there are hanging in the closet? Check out each and every room, pick up all the cloths (including out-of season clothing, coats, clothing in drawers, underwear, socks, costumes, uniforms, scarves, pajamas, loungewear) and throw them in a pile on your bed or bedroom. Empty your closet and through everything on the pile. It's huge! Aim to get rid of at least a quarter your clothing. Put favorite cloths back in your closet. Either hang them up or put them in the drawer. Put any piece of clothing you actually wear back in your closet. Put all the dirty cloths inside a clothes hamper. Cloths that you don't wear anymore will go into a bag to either consign or donate. Discard the cloths that are no longer useable. Get rid of the socks and underwear that are stretched out and frumpy. Go back to your closet and remove the old wire hangers and replace them with new ones. Now de-clutter your handbags, totes and clutches. Keep those you really love and discard the rest. De-clutter your shoes: get rid of the ones you no longer wear and the ones that are torn up and beyond repair. De-clutter the accessories.

- Next step is to de-clutter your kitchen. Do you have little snack stations all over the house? Everything food-related should go to the kitchen. Get a bag or box for items to be recycled. Check every room and put all the dirty dishes, cans, bags of chips to the kitchen and recycling area. De-clutter your car, and your working area. You can create a de-cluttering checklist to do it in a more organized fashion. Use your imagination to de-clutter objects that seem difficult to remove.

De-cluttering is not just about tossing the junks in the trash bag or sorting the items and arranging them in correct order. De-cluttering helps us to get a better understanding of things that matters in our life. It teaches us to let go the attachment of things that are burdensome and no longer serve us.

"MORNING IS AN IMPORTANT TIME OF DAY,
BECAUSE HOW YOU SPEND YOUR MORNING CAN
OFTEN TELL YOU WHAT KIND OF DAY YOU ARE
GOING TO HAVE." - LEMONY SNICKET

DAY TWO

A Perfect Routine

Do you know that the key to attaining your life goals is locked in your morning routine? If you start your day with a productive morning ritual, you can stay healthy and energetic throughout the day. A good morning ritual instills a sense of calm to start the day and helps you achieve a major goal by focusing on a single task.

Letting go the old staffs brought you a feeling of relief and satisfaction. You are feeling more focused, relaxed and productive now. It's the second day of your willpower challenge. Today we will create a powerful morning routine.

Creating a Morning Ritual

The morning routine should be simple and tailored to your unique circumstances and goals. A perfect routine will give you unstoppable willpower.

Morning is the most precious time of the day; but most of us wake slowly in the morning wasting the valuable minutes. Some of us take even an hour or more to drag ourselves out of bed. After getting out of bed, in the first hour, many of us pick activities that are against our goals. For instance, checking Facebook, twitter or other social media, watching television or cleaning up the messes (which could have been done last night). We choose activities that add zero value to our day. It may be because we don't know about the healthy morning ritual. The way we start our day affects the rest of it. Here are the basic rules we have to follow in order to create a good morning routine.

- Determine what time you'll get up in the morning. Waking up early in the morning positively impacts our day. Picking the time when you want to start your day depends on your current activities and responsibilities such as work, family, social circles and hobbies. Before deciding the hour when you want to wake up think the answers of the following questions:

1. How much time should you be spending getting ready in the morning?
2. What time do you drive your kids to school?
3. What time should you go to work?
4. How long do you travel to reach your workplace?

Find out how long it takes you to perform the above tasks. You have to start your day around one and half hour before you do all these things.

- For some of us, it can be difficult to change our entire routine in one day. In this case, you can start will small changes and gradually work your way up to your ideal morning routine. For instance, start with going to bed early and waking up early in the morning for the next few days. Once you've grown accustomed to this new time, introduce another small change such as going for a 30-minute jog everyday; and then add another change once it becomes a habit. The goal is to develop a series of habits that can bring positive changes in your life and become a natural part of your day. Here is an example:

Morning routine:

6:00AM: Waking up in the morning. Brush your teeth (2 minutes)

6:10AM: Drink water

6:12AM: Meditate

6:30AM: Go jogging

7:05AM: Shower

7:20AM: Breakfast+ Vitamin stack

7:30AM: Get ready to go to work

8:30AM: Arrive at the Office, Coffee/Tea

8:45AM: Write down ten ideas.

9:05AM: Work on the most important task

10:00AM: Check Email+ News

10:45AM: Check other tasks. Write down to-do list.

11:00AM: Work

As you can see, this routine looks pretty long. Following this same five-hour routine every morning may sound a bit strange, but it's worth it.

Your nighttime routine has an effect on your morning routine. Make sure to get enough sleep at night. An average adult needs between seven to nine hours of sleep every night, although every one of us has their unique sleep needs. Some may perform well on seven hours of sleep, while others might require nine hours to function optimally. If you don't get enough sleep at night, you will have extra hard time dealing with mornings. In order to improve your morning, you have to improve your sleep. Here are some tips for better sleep at night:

1. Increase your exposure to natural sunlight or bright light during day. Natural sunlight keeps our circadian rhythm (our body's natural time-keeping clock) healthy, which improves our quality of sleep.

2. Reduce your exposure to blue light in the evening. Blue light, which emits from electronic devices (smartphones, TV, laptop, iPad etc.), negatively impacts our circadian rhythm and can cause sleep problem. Therefore it is advised to stop watching TV and turn off any bright lights a couple of hours before sleep.

3. Avoid caffeine after 4:00 pm

4. Have your dinner at least a couple of hours before bedtime. If you have sensitive stomach, make it three hours.

5. You can include a long hot shower into your bedtime routine.

6. Begin all your nighttime responsibilities (e.g. doing the dishes, taking the trash,) a couple of hours before going to bed.

7. While it is important to avoid screen, listening to soothing music is a good idea. But avoid listening music that is too exiting or emotional.

8. While it is good to avoid caffeine and sugary drinks before bed, having a relaxing drink such as milk can help you sleep well

9. The peace and clarity of mind promotes sound sleep. If you find that engaging in spiritual activity brings you peace of mind, then it's a good idea for doing it before bedtime. Activities like doing light yoga, praying or reading spiritual literature brings a calming and positive feeling. You can also listen to a guided meditation or self-hypnosis recording.

10. If melatonin helps you sleep better, take it an hour before bed. But avoid sleeping pills if possible.

11. Turn off or cover all distracting lights in the room.

12. Lower the room temperature and use a weighted blanket.

Remember sleep-deprivation or having poor quality of sleep will make it difficult for us to generate and sustain willpower. We use the prefrontal cortex of our brain to exert willpower; lack of sleep negatively affects that area of the brain. Therefore it is important to have adequate amount of sleep every night.

"IF YOU'RE BORED WITH LIFE – YOU DON'T GET UP

EVERY MORNING WITH A BURNING DESIRE TO DO

THINGS – YOU DON'T HAVE ENOUGH GOALS."

– LOU HOLTZ

DAY THREE

Personal Goal-setting

Setting goals is not only about developing a roadmap for success and holding ourselves accountable, it is also about aligning ourselves with our deepest values and giving ourselves the motivation necessary to aim for things we never thought possible. We use our willpower to set goals, and when we succeed at one goal, it frees up our willpower so it can then be devoted to the next goal. This process also strengthens our willpower.

We already know that willpower is like a muscle. Just as untrained muscles tire out easily, untrained willpower fatigues too. Setting a realistic personal goal, staying focused and working on a timely manner to attain that goal, is a good way to build up our willpower muscle.

Goals give us focus. You may have all the potentials in the world, but without focus, the success will remain unobtainable. Setting goals will make you stretch beyond your usual self and reach new heights.

There are several stages of setting a powerful goal. In the first stage we will learn how to choose the right goal.

Choosing The Right Goal

We often daydream about what we want to accomplish in life. But most of us don't bother to write down the things we want to attain. If you pick up a pen and write down your dream on paper, it becomes concrete. Therefore the first step of goal setting is to write it down. If you are confused about what you want to achieve in life, use the following brainstorming technique:

Grab a pen and paper and write the topic you want to brainstorm in the form of a question on the top of the page. Ask yourself the question and, listen to all your answers. Write your answers down. Some of the answers may sound silly, embarrassing or impossible; write them down too. You're not going to share them with anyone. Listening to yourself is the first rule of brainstorming. Keep your pen moving for 5 minutes. Keep writing whatever pops into your mind. Keep writing until the time is up, and soon you will discover that you have something to say. Don't judge or criticize your ideas. Once you are done, bring another sheet of paper, and on the top, write:

What would I really want to accomplish in life if I were absolutely certain I would do it?

Again brainstorm the answers for five minutes. Once you're done, take a five-minute break. Stand up, stretch your hands; you can take a walk if you like. You have created two wish lists. After you come back, take a look into both lists. Now it is time to merge them into one.

Before choosing the ideas from the lists, let us know the characteristics of effective goals:

- A goal needs to be measurable, so that you can evaluate your progress and know when the goal is achieved. For instance, your goal is to lose 30 pounds bodyweight. You can program your diet and workouts accordingly, and measure the progress you're making. You will know when the goal is achieved.

- You should be able to visualize your goal. If you can picture yourself reaching your goals, it becomes easier to overcome the mental barrier and use the willpower to reach that goal.

- Goal should be realistic or achievable. Your goal should challenge your skill and abilities, but it must not discourage your effort and performance.

- Your goal should have a realistic deadline. Setting a realistic timeframe is important to design an action plan. For example, if we set a timeframe of 3 months to lose 30 pound weight, we can design a nutrition and exercise plan to reach that goal within that timeframe. A timeframe motivates to you faster and produce better results. Schedule enough time to reach your goal, but not so much time that you lose interest in it.

- To achieve bigger goals, we need to divide them into small manageable parts. Because for most of us bigger goals can be overwhelming. Therefore before picking your goals, make sure they are manageable.

- After setting a goal, we create an action plan. For the purpose of developing steps, a goal should be analyzed for potential problems that might keep us from reaching it. To minimize the errors, we need to cover all angles. Therefore it is important to learn what could go wrong, so that we can plan in advance to tackle that problem.

- Your goal must yield rewards that will benefit you. The reward has to be something that motivates your effort to achieve the goal.

Now you know the characteristics of effective goals. Use the above criteria to pick items from both lists and rank them from most important to least important.

Now you have a list of SMART (specific, measurable, achievable, realistic and timely) personal goals.

"I WOULD VISUALIZE THINGS COMING TO ME. IT

WOULD JUST MAKE ME FEEL BETTER.

VISUALIZATION WORKS IF YOU WORK HARD.

THAT'S THE THING. YOU CAN'T JUST VISUALIZE

AND GO EAT A SANDWICH."

- JIM CARREY

DAY FOUR

Visualization Tool for Channeling Willpower

In the second step of goal setting, we will use a visualization tool to channel our willpower more productively as we work toward our goals. We will create a vision board, which will help us to harness our mental energy and encourage us to put more effort into achieving the goal at hand. This tool will allow us to define our goals with inspirational images that will motivate us along our journey. A vision board is undeniably effective, because it trains us to stay focused on our goals.

Creating a Vision Board

There are no hard and fast rules for creating a vision board and everyone has a personal way of designing it. Therefore create your vision board on your own terms. Making physical boards out of poster-board, corkboard or any material is a popular idea. But you can also make a digital version if you like by creating a private file in your computer.

First think about your future goals from personal growth, career, finances and relationships to education, social life or spiritual growth. Now envision what you want each of the areas to look like. Allow yourself to spend a stress free hour to put your board together.

Create a relaxing environment when you are making your vision board. Turn on some soothing music and light a candle if you like. You may experience clutters clouding your mind... take time and allow your mind to settle down. Now start putting your staffs on the board.

Add images that represent your goal— photos of cars you want to drive, travel destinations you want to visit, house you want to live… you may also add your favorite quotes. Use scissors, tape, pins or glue stick to put your board together. You can cut images or quotes from magazines; use fun markers, stickers or any other staffs you think to deck out your board.

You may also include the images of your memorable past events like photos of vacations, marriage ceremony, convocation and so forth. Anything that inspires you, add in your board.

Place your vision board somewhere you can see it everyday…in this way you will prompt yourself to visualize your goal on a regular basis. Update your board whenever it feels right but don't forget to look at your vision board every day.

"WHATEVER WE PLANT IN OUR SUBCONSCIOUS MIND AND NOURISH WITH REPETITION AND EMOTION WILL ONE DAY BECOME A REALITY."

- EARL NIGHTINGALE

DAY FIVE

Your Vision and The Subconscious Mind

A goal is a specially created milestone where you intend to reach. A vision is the big picture of your intended result. Spending time with vision board will give you the motivation to move toward your goal. But in order to promote self-belief, you have to practice "creative visualization" exercise. Creative visualization or guided imagery is actually a meditation to visualize yourself accomplishing your goals. The aim of this exercise is to move your thought from conscious mind to your subconscious mind.

Our subconscious mind is the reservoir of enormous amount of knowledge. It is the second layer of human mind that governs our waking moments, controls our behaviors and actions. But this level of mind can't distinguish the reality from vivid imagination. Therefore, if we place a realistic picture before the subconscious mind, the mind will believe in it and work tirelessly to bring that image into reality.

Practicing Creative Visualization

To practice creative visualization, find a quiet corner of a room, where you can sit comfortably and won't be disturbed for the next twenty minutes. Turn-off your phone or put it into silent mode. Lock the door and close the window to reduce the noise level. Wear comfortable clothing.

Now sit down. Close your eyes; Think about a goal from the wish list you've created.

Take a deep slow breath through your nose and exhale slowly. Spend more time in exhaling. Take few more deep breaths and allow yourself to relax deeply with each out-breath.

Now imagine yourself sitting in a quiet room in a large comfortable white chair—deeply nestled and completely relaxed. There is a large interactive video screen in front of you, and a 10-second countdown has started on the projected screen— 9...8...7...6...5...4...3...2...1...0

Now visualize that your future life is being projected on the screen. Picture yourself achieving your goal. Vividly imagine what you want the future to look like when you get there. For instance, you can watch yourself walking across the stage, being congratulated by the CEO, and enjoying your moment in the spotlight.

If your aim is to achieve a fitness goal, you can imagine yourself eating nourishing foods. Feel that you have a strong metabolic system, and the food you are eating supports your muscular growth and keeps your body healthy and fit. You can also visualize yourself in the gym. Vividly imagine the environment of your gym and the instruments like racks of dumbbells, stakes of iron plates, rows of machines; Imagine yourself performing each exercise: every set and every rep. Imagine the flawless execution; feel the sweat, the burn in your muscles, the pace of your breathing, the way weights feel in your grips. Imagine your body is gradually transforming into the perfect shape as you are performing the workouts. Finally visualize participating in social events and people admiring your new look.

You can visualize any of your goals. Visualization is more effective if you participate as a first person.

Make sure not to meditate to the point of mental fatigue, strain or boredom— 15 to 20 minutes should be enough. Practice this exercise every day in the morning or at night before you go to bed.

When you are done with visualization, take a few deep breaths, and gently open your eyes.

"A GOAL WITHOUT A PLAN IS JUST A WISH."

- ANTOINE DE SAINT-EXUPÉRY

DAY SIX

Your Action Steps

An action plan will help us to get where we need to go. We have already set our personal goals. Now we will break the long-term goals into small and easier-to-accomplish ones and work our way up to the big goal. By creating action steps, we are trying to make sure that our actions and decisions are oriented towards achieving our goals.

An ideal action plan consists of many small steps to accomplish on the way to our goal. Each step offers a new challenge, and when we accomplish one step, we gain confidence and willpower to work on the next step.

Creating An Effective Plan

Our today's task is to develop an action plan. We will start with listing the tasks (action steps) that we need to carry out to attain our objectives. Then we will analyze the tasks to create an effective plan.

In order to design an action plan, here are the steps you have to follow:

- Grab a pen and paper and write the letter "A" on left hand side and the letter "B" on the right hand side of the paper. Draw a straight line from A to B. You are ready to create your timeline, which will eventually become your action plan.

- Pick a goal from your wish list. Then brainstorm all the tasks you need to accomplish to reach your goal. Write down every single task you think you might need to take to accomplish your objective.

- Once done, look at the list and eliminate the similar ideas. Now you may be left with 5 to 7 steps.

- What is the very first action you need to take? After the completion of first step what comes next? Find out the answers. Find out if there is any step that should be prioritized to meet specific deadlines.

Now we will arrange the items in order. Place the first step next to the "A" you drew. Then place the second step next to the first step...then the next step. Every single step has to be in correct order.

- Now that you can see your entire project from beginning to end, look at each step in greater detail. Is there any step that you can skip and still meet your objective? Or is there any step you think should be added? It is ok to make change if necessary.

Although it is nice to believe that that your schedule will run smoothly, your project is a subject to opportunities and threats. While opportunities have the potentials to benefit you, threats can harm your project and keep you from achieving your goals. For instance, your goal is to get promoted in your job. The threat on this project might be that a lot of other people may have an interest to obtain the same position. On the other hand, an opportunity might appear when you hear that someone has left a position and it's the job you want. In the next session, we will learn how to analyze the risks.

"RISK COMES FROM NOT KNOWING WHAT YOU'RE

DOING." - WARREN BUFFETT

DAY SEVEN

The Risk Factors

Accessing your risk is something like budgeting for the downside. If you utilize the risk factors, it will help you to take a thoughtful and calculated approach.

Today we will discuss about analyzing and managing risks to achieve our goals. There are two major risks — one is opportunity risk and another is threat risk. The problem with risk is that you can't measure the chance of an event occurring and exactly what it might cost if the risk really occurs. You have to approximate, and that makes the risk decision more complex. For instance, if the likelihood of small financial impact is moderate, you won't be interested to spend much time and money on it. However, if there is a greater likelihood of a big financial impact, you may want to spend a good amount of money to meet that risk

Making The Risk Decision

As every situation is unique, you have to be careful in decision-making. Ask yourself the following questions before taking the risk decisions:

1. What's the best that can happen, if I make this decision?
2. What's the worst that can happen, if I make this decision?
3. Is number one worth risking number two?
4. Can I live with number two if it happens?

We only have a few strategies that we can use to manage our risks, whether it's a threat risk or opportunity risk. Here are some general strategies for both risks:

Active and passive acceptance (for both risks): Only deal with the risk when it really occurs. Develop a contingency plan and apply it when necessary.

Three strategies for Threat risk: There are three methods you can apply to deal with threat risk. The first method is "avoidance", where you change the plan so that the risk can't happen or have a zero impact. The second method is transfer, where you can transfer the risk to someone else. The third method is mitigation, where you can lower the risk instead of eliminating it or giving it to somebody. Here is an example:

Avoidance: A care home is installing an elevator to eliminate the hazard of falling down the stirs.

Transfer: The care home is purchasing an insurance policy that would cover any injuries sustained from a client falling down the stirs.

Mitigate: The care home is installing lighting signs, and handrails to minimize the likelihood that someone will fall down the stirs.

Three strategies for opportunity risk: The first method is "enhancing", where you can increase the probability impact to turn a small opportunity into a big one. The second method is "exploitation", which means to take actions to ensure the opportunity will be realized. The third method is "sharing", which implies that that you may offer to lend a hand to someone else to share the benefit and save time. This approach is more useful when the benefit is worth more to someone else than it is to you. Here is an example:

You are constructing a building and your client is offering you a monetary reward if you can complete the task 3 months earlier than planned. You can consider the following three strategies:

Enhancement: You are taking some measures to shorten the duration of the project. Although it is not going to cost you any extra money, it can increase the risk of possible rework or future delays.

Exploitation: You are taking practical measures to complete the project ahead of time. Such as motivating your team to perform faster, introducing overtime and offering rewards if they manage to complete the project 3 months before the actual completion date.

Sharing: You are partnering up with someone whom you have offered a share of profit for investing money into your project, so that you can cover the extra cost for completing the project ahead of time.

"THE GAME OF LIFE IS A LOT LIKE FOOTBALL.

YOU HAVE TO TACKLE YOUR PROBLEMS, BLOCK

YOUR FEARS, AND SCORE YOUR POINTS WHEN

YOU GET THE OPPORTUNITY."

- LEWIS GRIZZARD

DAY EIGHT

When The Problems Arise

Obtaining a big goal not easy. If reaching goals were easy, everyone would do it quickly and without any problem. As you take the first step towards your goal, you never know what you may encounter on the way. Sometime unexpected problems can come your way and derail you. Don't let them deviate you from the course of your goal. You've developed an effective action plan and assessed your risks. Your vision is clear and you can articulate the intended outcome in detail, but there are always obstacles in the path. These obstacles may come in different flavors. Some of them can be much bigger than others. But regardless of the nature, of the size, the obstacle you might be facing can be handled efficiently by applying the right problem solving strategy.

Find your strength in the face of adversity, and use your problem solving skill to clear your obstacles. Removing the obstacles may not be easy, but it is wonderfully gratifying. Today we will learn how to deal with obstacles.

Dealing With Obstacles

The first step to overcome any obstacle is to define it. There is an old saying— "A problem well-defined is a problem half-solved". This saying indicates the notion that if we take time to fully comprehend the nature of our obstacle, overcoming the obstacle will take less time and effort. By seeing the complete picture of your problem, you can see the solution.

Defining the obstacle is like identifying a roadmap of our destination. In order to set the appropriate goal we need to have the clear idea about the challenge at hand whether it's a career problem or relationship issue or other life's challenges. Here are the five steps of defining a challenge:

1. Looking for available facts
2. Explaining the facts clearly
3. Distinguishing facts from assumptions
4. Identifying the factors to overcome.

Looking for available facts: We often try to solve a problem without having a clear idea of the facts. But enquiring about the facts is critical for any problem solving.

Therefore look for the facts; dig deeper. Seek the answers of following questions. If any of the questions are not applicable to your situation, skip them and move to the next question:

When does this problem occur?

How exactly does it occur?

When does it not happen?

Why does it not happen during these times?

Does anything change during these times?

Are you doing anything differently?

The main purpose of learning the answer is to find the exception times. These are the times when the challenges we are facing, do not happen for one reason or another. Solution of our problem may lie within these exception times. Our next job is to focus on the consequence of the problem. Ask yourself the following questions:

In which way are the outcomes of this problem felt?

What could happen if nothing is done about the problem or the problem is ignored?

If the problem brings negative outcomes, what could potentially lead to those outcomes?

How this negative outcome could affect your life and the life of others?

If the problem is resolved, could it beget other problems? Why or why not?

Explaining the facts clearly: When we are overwhelmed by challenges, we feel stressed and tend to use language that is unclear. Therefore when we answer the questions we have to describe the facts as clearly as we can. When we can't explain something clearly, we often blow things out of proportion.

Distinguishing facts from assumptions: Sometimes when people use emotional tools to deal with their challenges, they make assumptions without paying attention to the automatic thought process. An assumption involves an individual's beliefs or interpretations without determining its validity. If all of our actions are based on assumptions, our problem solving attempts are likely to fail. Therefore prior to working on unverified information, you have to separate facts from assumptions. Ask yourself the following questions:

What are the possible assumptions you might be making about your problem?

How do you think these assumptions contributing to your problem?

How this problem is perceived by someone close to you?

Do you know someone who has successfully overcome this problem before?

What can you learn from that person?

Identifying the factors you have to overcome: Set realistic problem solving goals. If your problem-solving goal seems unattainable, you are setting yourself up for defeat. For instance, setting the goal of attaining financial independence within a year is likely to be out of reach for most people. However, setting a goal of decreasing your overall expenses in order to save and additional 5% of our salary by next year seems quite manageable. People often set emotion-focused goals rather than problem focused goals. Goals that are problem focused have objectives that involve altering the nature of a situation so that it is no longer a problem. Emotion focused goals don't offer solutions to your problems.

Once the problem-solving goal is set, identify the factors that are preventing you from reaching that goal. Create a plan and eliminate those factors.

"HE WHO ANGERS YOU CONQUERS YOU."

- ELIZABETH KENNY

DAY NINE

Willpower VS Self Control

Willpower and self-control both refer to the same mental processes, although there is a difference between these two. Self-control is about intentionally controlling your urges and behaviors. We use our self-control when we refrain ourselves from doing something that's morally bad. For instance when someone deliberately resists the urge of smoking, he exercises self-control. Willpower is the power of your will. When you are determined to reach your goal and motivate yourself to do whatever it takes to obtain it, you're using your willpower.

The mental power you are using to control your urge and the power you use to reach your goal are not different.

That's why when you exercise self-control, you're actually exercising your willpower.

Practicing self-control is critical for success because the process of self-control involves managing emotions. Controlling emotions is important. Because when the emotion takes over, reason flies out of the window and we take unproductive decisions.

Self-control is about protecting yourself against yourself. It is about resisting temptation and moving ahead to achieve long-term goals. Practicing self-control will give you a sense of mastery over your life, and eliminate the feeling of helplessness and insecurity. It will improve your self-esteem, confidence and willpower to push through anything.

Building Self-control

Today we will learn how to develop long-term self-control. There are many ways to boost self-control. But in this chapter we will strengthen our self-control by breaking bad habits. This will not just clear some major obstacles to success, but build our perseverance and give our willpower a boost.

Bad habits can negatively affect your health, performance, career growth and hold you back from success Changing bad habits takes persistence and the right mindset.

The first step of changing any bad habit is to identify it. List the bad habits you want to change, which may include everything from biting nails to overspending. Pick a negative habit from your list such as smoking or eating junk foods. Now think about the situational and emotional context that triggers that bad habit. Situations that trigger the craving for smoking or eating unhealthy foods can be the situations that cause stress or boredom. Write down when you mostly feel the impulse to smoke or eat junk foods. Write few notes about how you feel and what you think when you experience the urge. Or you can maintain a thought diary. Here is the simple structure for a thought diary:

Colum 1: Situation

Identify the moment when the craving surfaces. Did you feel stressed when you experienced the craving or was there any other reason why the cravings occur?

Column 2: How do you feel?

Express your feeling in one word, like angry, sad, or frustrated.

Column 3: Negative thoughts

Identify the negative thoughts that bring forth the bad feeling or thoughts closely related to bad feeling (if the bad feeling triggers the urge of eating unhealthy or smoking)

Column 4: Rate your moods

In this final stage, go back to your moods in column 2 and re-rate them.

Where I am now	Emotion Or Feeling	Negative thought	My mood score

A trigger is any form of stimuli that initiates the desire to fall into the bad habit. In order to manage the triggers of bad habits, first you have to identify them. Before you start the " identifying the trigger exercise", there are few things you need to consider:

You may need to make some lifestyle changes to break-free from bad habits. Here some areas of your life where you may need some change:

Availability: If the triggers of your negative habits are readily available, you may need to change your environment.

Activities: If you spend a considerable amount of time involving in that behavior, you may need to look for other ways to spend your time.

Relationships with peers: If the people you mix with contribute to maintaining your negative habits, you may need to limit the time you spend with them.

Exercise

- Give a brief description of two situations that triggered your negative habit

   Trigger situation 1:...............................

   Trigger situation 2...................................

- Now describe the consequences normally related with this situation (both negative and positive consequences)

Negative consequence of trigger situation 1:...........

Negative consequences of trigger situation 2:..........

- Next step is to develop new choices in the trigger situations you've described.

Describe two choices and their probable consequences for your first trigger situation. For each choice, briefly describe what would happen if you made that choice.

Possible consequences of choice 1:......................

Possible consequences of choice 2:......................

- After describing the possible consequences, our task is to explain what need to be done to obtain those choices. Therefore briefly describe how you could put your choice into practice.

Choice 1: Change plan

Choice 2: Change plan.

Remember changing the old negative habits takes great commitment. If you don't see the problem you won't find mental strength to change your behavior. The more honest you are with yourself about the nature of your negative habit, the more likely you'll take measures to break your bad habits.

A bad habit takes years to develop. You can't just shake them off in an instant. Therefore be patient and don't try to change too much at once. Start small and gradually increase until you get the desired result. Maintain a diary or journal to record your progress to keep yourself motivated. However, despite your best effort, you may experience occasional relapse, which is quite normal. If it happens, find out why you slipped. Record the incident in your diary. You can carry around "coping cards" with you. These small cards may contain positive statements, motivational quotes, distraction techniques, breathing exercises and other techniques. You can prevent a relapse by gaining motivation by looking at the coping cards. However if you experience relapses very often, you may need additional support.

"WE ARE WHAT WE REPEATEDLY DO.

EXCELLENCE, THEN, IS NOT AN ACT, BUT A

HABIT." - WILL DURANT

DAY TEN

Habit Replacement

You've already learned how to eliminate bad habits. But in order to stay goal oriented, you also have to establish some good habits.

We humans are creatures of habit. And that's why changing the lifestyle is hard. Some people make commitment strategies to develop a positive habit. It is a good idea to keep themselves accountable, but this technique is not always effective. Some habits can be quite challenging to develop, such as transitioning to a vegan lifestyle. If the habit is too big, you may need to break it into small steps, and gradually boost your self-efficacy.

Today is the 9th day of our willpower challenge. In this session we will learn how to use our willpower to build good habits.

Forming Good Habits

Breaking bad habits are important; because bad habit takes us away from our goal and harm other areas of our lives. But in order to maintain the progress, quitting negative habits is not enough— we have to replace bad habits with good habits. For instance if your goal is to lose weight and get lean, giving up junk food is not enough, you have to replace this with healthy diets. If you have a negative habit of spending too much time on social media, simply limiting the time is not enough. You have to utilize the time doing something productive, such as learning piano or reading books.

We already introduced some good habits in our willpower program. However every time we break a bad habit, it is important that we replace it with a healthy habit.

Here is how to establish a new habit that'll stick.

First thing we have to do to develop a habit is to be aware. That means we have to examine our habits, and find out what new habit we need to introduce. Then we will make the decision and commitment to make changes. This is not always easy. How many times we said to ourselves, "Yes, I should wake up early in the morning, do some workouts and eat healthy. Not to worry, I'll get around it, sooner or later." Then we procrastinate and the change never happens because procrastination just makes it harder. In order to get the wheels of motion in action, you'll need conscious commitment. Make sure that what you want to change is something you feel you really want to change and you really need to change. You're unlikely to accomplish a change, if you truly don't feel that you need it and it is not keeping with your values.

If the change is big, you have to start small. To make room for your new habit, find out what you'll be adding or subtracting from your daily routine.

Develop behavior chains. Use your current routine to build environment "triggers" that will let you know when to act on your new habit. This strategy is also known as "implement intentions", which involves picking an existing habit and building a link with the new habit.

For instance, you want to develop a habit of cleaning your house everyday. If you aim for cleaning your room/kitchen every evening after you come home and change your cloths, it will be more easier because you're linking it with a regular part of your schedule. You're building an environmental trigger that will tell you when to practice your new habit.

Make a plan. Avoid fantasizing about the result. You can use visualization technique (day five) described in the book to overcome the mental barriers. New habits can be fragile. Therefore you must ignore the negative self-talks that tell you "it's not worth the effort!". Use positive affirmations to stay motivated. You may also find a healthy way to reward yourself for successfully acting on the change for a week or two.

A change takes a while to become part of your behavior, to become a habit. I will say it's the 90-day mark. The longer you stick to the change, the more likely it will become automatic. Anything you do consistently for a long period of time becomes a habit. And once the habit is formed, you no longer need to put much effort into it.

"THE KEY TO WINNING IS POISE UNDER STRESS."

- PAUL BROWN

DAY ELEVEN

The Negative Effects of Stress

It is important to stay calm under pressure as you work toward your goal. Remaining stress free can help you perform well and make better decisions at work. Although stress can push you to perform better and stimulate your brain to cope with challenging situations, too much stress can make you anxious and destroy your productivity. It can also create many health problems.

When your stress creates the sense of urgency to complete your task on time, then that stress is a positive force. But when your stress turns your performance in a life and death situation, then it's a negative force that can diminish your focus, decision-making and performance. When Stress negatively affects your performance, health and productivity, you have apply de-stressing techniques to stay calm and in control. Use the following exercise to de-stress your mind and body.

Relieving Stress

There are many stress relieving techniques available today. Progressive relaxation is one of the powerful de-stressing methods that can effectively calm your body and mind. To try this technique, sit or lie down in a comfortable position. Make sure you are wearing loose clothing. Here are the steps to follow.

1. When you are ready, take a slow deep breath and let your stomach to expand. Then exhale slowly. Do it couple more times.

2. Now press your knees together to tighten your thighs. Hold the tension for the count of eight. Then release... Notice that your leg muscles are more relaxed. Pause for five seconds

3. As you tighten and relax your muscles, become aware of the difference between the muscles when they're tensed and when they are relaxed. Tighten the muscles of your buttock by pulling together.

Hold the tension and count from one to eight. Then release. Allow relaxation to slowly replace your tension. Take a five second break.

4. Gently tighten your stomach muscles by sucking-in, but do not strain. Hold for eight seconds. Then let go. You feel total relaxation in this area. Relax for five seconds.

5. Now clench your fists and draw your both forearms toward your shoulders. Tighten your biceps and keep the pressure for eight seconds and release. Pause for five seconds.

6. Clench your fists again— now more firmly. Hold the tension while counting eight. Then slowly allow the fingers to release one by one until they are completely relaxed. Stay relaxed for five seconds.

7. Now take a deep breath and tighten your chest. Maintain the pressure for eight seconds... then release. And relax for five seconds.

8. Contract your upper back by making your shoulder blades closer. Stay in this position for eight seconds then release. Relax for five seconds. Now lift your shoulders up closer to your ears.

Hold to the count of eight. As you release, feel that the tension melts away as you loosen up the shoulder muscles.

9. Remember to breathe naturally as you do this exercise. Bring your head back so that your chin points upward. Hold to the count of eight and release.

10. Finally contract your facial muscles: open your mouth wide enough to stretch the hinges of your jaw. Hold for eight seconds and release. Squint your eyelids tightly shut and tighten your eye muscles.... after eight seconds, let go.

Smile as widely as you can and tighten your cheek muscles. Hold for eight seconds... release.

Lift your eyebrows to tighten the muscles in you forehead.... Count eight and let go.

As you progressively tense and relax different parts of your body, make sure not to hurt yourself by applying too much pressure. If you still feel tense, repeat the procedure one more time.

"IT'S YOUR REACTION TO ADVERSITY, NOT ADVERSITY ITSELF THAT DETERMINES HOW YOUR LIFE'S STORY WILL DEVELOP."

– DIETER F. UCHTDORF

DAY TWELVE

Emotional Resilience and Relapse Management

Sometimes our uncomfortable inner-experiences (a thought, emotion, craving) force us to give up on our willpower goal. But if we want to reach our willpower goal, we have to train our ability to tolerate our uncomfortable inner experiences. Paradoxically the best way to do this is to learn how to experience the uncomfortable inner-experience more fully.

As you move on with your new habits, you may experience a strong urge to go back to your old habit. Unwittingly you can slip back into a bad habit you've just given up. We call this "relapse". Relapse occurs when you fall back into your former state of being. For instance, after a period of sobriety when a former alcoholic takes his first sip, his relapse starts.

In this session we will know how to develop emotional tolerance to deal with the feeling of craving and other painful emotions like frustration, sadness and anxiety. This will not just help us to prevent relapse and build emotional resilience but also to develop greater willpower and self-control.

Tolerating Emotional Discomfort

Emotional discomfort, not surprisingly can be painful. When we experience emotional discomfort, we resist, judge, or run away from this feeling in hopes of avoiding the ache. We try to numb the discomfort may be with a glass of wine or three. We may even hurt ourselves or engage in other kinds of self-harm. We try everything we can do to reduce our discomfort. But our attempts to alleviate the discomfort only reinforce to ourselves that we can't handle distress. And the paradox is that by doing this things, we only make our situation worse. Things we usually do to minimize the emotional discomforts actually amplify it in the long run. For instance self-harm may provide some level of relief in the short term. However in the long run it only spikes stress. It may bring a sense of guilt or shame as people try to stop this behavior.

People who enjoy a high quality of life make attempts to tolerate their emotional discomfort as opposed to avoiding it. Learning to tolerate emotional pain will help you to stand up to emotional distress. It will also prevent relapse and help you to maintain the changes you're making.

To build emotional tolerance, spend some time every day to sit with your emotions. Notice what you're experiencing without judging or criticizing your feeling. For instance, you're experiencing frustration as you're not satisfied with the rate of progress in reaching your life goal. This frustration accompanies other emotions life fear, anger, self-loathing and guilt. Instead of fighting the feeling or telling yourself that you "cant' stand" this feeling, allow it enter into your mind. Experience it wholly. Notice as it ebbs and flows. Let the feelings come and go— don't resist them.

Validate your emotion. If you're feeling angry, say to yourself, "this is anger". If the feeling is guilt, say to yourself, "this is guilt". But don't criticize the feeling or fight the feeling. The goal with emotion is to be able to go wherever they lead you and experience every emotion that comes in the way, without judging them. Don't try to change anything or feel a certain way.

As you sit with your painful emotion of frustration and accept the feeling the way it is, say to yourself, "It makes sense that I'm feeling hurt because I'm not satisfied with the progress. It's quite OK to feel this way".

If it is the feeling of craving of alcohol or junk food, say to yourself, "I'm feeling an urge to drink or eat unhealthy foods, which is normal. But I'm taking my life in my own hands. I don't need to consume unhealthy staffs to feel good and be in peace with myself. I'm able to stay in control".

If you're not experiencing any negative feeling, stay with your present feeling, and observe as each feeling appears, peaks and disappears. Spend 10 minutes with your emotions everyday.

Accepting the feeling the way they are will relieve the discomfort and boost your emotional tolerance.

Willpower is related to the allowance of discomfort and the delay of gratification. The more willing you are to feel uncomfortable, the more you can develop this quality. Therefore learn to embrace the uncomfortable emotions and feelings to achieve your long-term goals.

"LIFE ISN'T MEANT TO BE LIVED PERFECTLY...BUT MERELY TO BE LIVED. BOLDLY, WILDLY, BEAUTIFULLY, UNCERTAINLY, IMPERFECTLY, MAGICALLY LIVED."

- MANDY HALE

DAY THIRTEEN

The Inevitability of Making Mistakes

Making mistakes may be unpleasant, but it is inevitable in everyone's life. None of us are perfect; we all make mistakes; it's written into our biology that we will make them. We learn through our mistakes. It's OK to make mistakes sometimes and if you're lucky enough, the mistakes can be fixed. While mistakes can help you to grow as a person, continually regretting for mistakes will deplete your willpower. Therefore we have to recover from our mistakes and move on. Today we'll learn how to bounce back from our mistakes.

Recovering From Mistakes

If we had superpower we would undo every mistakes we made in life. The feeling of defeat is awful. It drains your self-esteem, makes you feel like you're carrying a heavy burden on your shoulders. But if you are constantly obsessed about what happened and beat yourself up for your mistake, you're preparing yourself for more defeat. It is in your best interest to limit the damage from your mistakes, and learn from it as much as possible. You have to get past your frustration, guilt to move forward.

After making a mistake, most of us fall into one of two camps: those with fixed mindset thinks that they will be never good at this, and those with growth-mindset views that mistake as a "wake-up call". They figure out what went wrong then adapt accordingly.

Research shows that the best way to learn from mistake is to embrace the string of failure. Discover the benefits and lessons within your mistakes. The mistakes we make don't come with a log file and stack trace. But they surely come with lessons. Therefore take a magnifying glass to your slop up and find out where things went wrong. Determine what exactly caused the error. You may realize there are patterns in your performance that contribute to that error. Once you identify the pattern, you can work on ways to fix that pattern. Create a plan for how you'll avoid similar mistakes in the future. Don't lose the lessons.

Own your errors.

Accept your fault right away because ethical people don't hesitate to own up their mistakes. After you've made a mistake, the worst thing you can do is attempt to sweep it under the rug and pretend that nothing happened. Don't always be a "quiet fixer". Errors may often have side affects, and pretending that it did not happen can bring negative consequences. If anyone is affected by your mistake, make a real apology; don't make lame and self-protective statements. After apologies are made, your next step will be to find out whether you can do anything to remedy your fault. This may involve some extra work on your plate. But your apologies are pointless if you're not keen to accept the consequences.

Making mistakes is the part of the process of becoming better. Remember, mistakes are there to guide you, not define you.

The final step of recovering from your mistake is to let go and move on. But it is not easy for many of us. Remember being constantly obsessed over your failure and shortcomings won't do you any failure; it will rather prevent you from being productive and generate more failures. Do everything you can to recover your mistake. And once you're done, smooth things up by taking a deep breath and move on with a clear head. You don't want the "stomach in our shoes" feeling when you know that you've done a big mistake. It does not matter how bad you feel about your fault, what matters is how you bounce back from it.

"LIVE AND WORK, BUT DO NOT FORGET TO PLAY –

TO HAVE FUN IN LIFE AND REALLY ENJOY IT."

- EILEEN CADDY

DAY FOURTEEN

Willpower Recharge

Staying focused and continuously working on your goal is definitely critical for attaining success. But sometimes you've to take a break to acknowledge your small accomplishments and recharge your willpower. This technique involves rewarding yourself for achieving small action steps. Today we will learn about the benefits of rewarding ourselves for small success and how to recharge our willpower by celebrating our wins.

Celebrating Small Success And Rewarding Yourself

You're exercising your willpower muscle as you're working hard to achieve your goal. It can be a long and difficult process. You may experience challenges and setbacks, and at some point you may feel that it's just too high a mountain to climb. This happens when you tend to focus on the end goal rather than the small and significant steps you take to reach there. Focusing intently on outcomes may lead two negative results: the first is the process seems to be overwhelming; it just seems too much to bother trying. The second is that you attempt to do many things at once, but none of them seem very meaningful or satisfying. But in order to actualize your goal, you have to put more focus on the immediate task, the smaller goal. You have to take one step at a time, celebrate your success for every small win.

Remember, big goals don't happen overnight. When you're setting a big goal, you're actually assigning yourself for hundreds of small tasks, and you have to accomplish those tasks in order to reach the end goal.

If you fail to acknowledge the small successes, you'll end up diminishing your motivation, and motivation is what keeps us on the right path, gives us the strength to move forward.

Celebrate small wins and reward yourself every week or once every couple of weeks. The more you acknowledge and reward yourself for your successes, the more success will you attain. By taking time to acknowledge your actions, you are actually strengthening those actions. You're connecting the positive emotions with small achievements, and making success a habit.

Remember, "What gets rewarded, gets repeated". Rewards are incentives for yourself to stay motivated and become a stronger willed person. Making time everyday or week, for reflecting on all those moments of success will bring immense joy to your life. Contrarily if you fail to acknowledge and reward your success, you're creating a negative cycle. Your subconscious mind will start to think, "what's the point of doing this!" because you're not obtaining any pleasure from it.

There are many ways to reward the success. If you're scratching your head how to reward yourself, here is a list of ideas:

1. Take yourself out to breakfast or lunch

2. Buy something that makes you happy, like a new picture-frame for your desk or an electronic Day-Timer.

3. Listen to music that inspires you.

4. Go to a carnival or festival.

5. Dance

6. Take a nap

7. Attend a sporting event

8. Play a sport

9. See a movie.

10. Watch funny videos on YouTube

11. Play your favorite online game

12. Go swimming

13. Get a manicure and/or pedicure

14. Get yourself a massage

15. Treat yourself to a facial

16. Plan a night out with your friends.

17. Take a day trip to an interesting place of attraction in your area, like a theme park, zoo or aquarium.

18. Read a novel you can't put down

19. Throw a party

20. Go for a bike ride.

Don't indulge in the negative habits you've given up to reward your success. While rewarding yourself will recharge your willpower, overdoing it may weaken it. Therefore make sure not to overdo anything.

"IF YOU PUT OFF EVERYTHING TILL YOU'RE SURE

OF IT, YOU'LL NEVER GET ANYTHING DONE."

– NORMAN VINCENT PEALE

DAY FIFTEEN

Procrastination: The Enemy of Productivity

Making the best use of time is critical for reaching your goal. In order to reach the big goal, you have to achieve all the small steps in a timely manner. You can't just delay or postpone any task because you're not in the mood. If you put off impending tasks for later time, and frequently miss deadlines, you may fall into the trap of procrastination.

Procrastination is an enemy of success and productivity, a vicious force that prevents you from following through on what you set out to do. A single act of procrastination can lead you to the procrastination doom loop that keeps you procrastinating forever.

Wasting time and not meeting deadlines can have a devastating effect on your personal and professional life. In the long run this harmful tendency can take a steep toll on your potential, finances and even your health. If you find yourself constantly delaying the important tasks and struggling to meet deadlines, then you're having procrastination problem, which you must overcome if you want to succeed at accomplishing your goal.

Establishing Control Over Procrastination

Various methods can be applied to establish control over procrastination. Optimal performance method is one of the powerful strategies that can be used to override procrastination impulses.

There are three stages of optimal performance method: relaxation, mobilization and action.

Let us start with relaxation.

In order to relax your mind and body, listen calming music or take a warm bath or imagine a peaceful and serene place. You may also try breathing exercises, meditation or progressive relaxation techniques.

Once you feel relaxed and calm, enter into the next phase, "Mobilization".

In the mobilization stage, take time to recall the memories of times where you acted efficiently. Think what you did when tempted to procrastination. Think how you ignored the temptation and continued to maintain full focus on the task at hand.

Whatever the event of success you've picked, this is your optimal performance experience. Reconstructing this moment in your mind helps you to connect it to the mental and visceral states relating to that experience. How did it make you feel? What sensations did you experience? This is a mobilizing feeling that prepares you to launch an action. Now move to the action phase.

When you're in the action phase, you'll create a positive déjà vu experience by recalling the optimal experience, which will motivate you to take action.

Use this motivation and willpower to resist your urge of "task aversion" and bring the best out of you.

"I THINK THE HARDEST PART OF AGING REALLY

IS RECOGNIZING THE TIME THAT YOU WASTED

AND THE THINGS THAT YOU WORRIED ABOUT

THAT REALLY DIDN'T MATTER.... THAT'S REALLY

THE ONLY REGRET THAT I HAVE."

- OPRAH WINFREY

DAY SIXTEEN

Effective Time Management

Procrastination ruins your spirit, mutes your dreams and dulls your senses and getting rid of it is a big success. But in order to become a goal achiever, you also have to learn how to use time wisely.

Remember success is a choice. The people who are most successful, choose to be successful with their powerful willpower. They set clear goals, utilize their time wisely, and work consistently toward their goal. The super achievers never waste their time. They also don't waste their effort. They know how to enjoy their time and remain productive at the same time. They don't worry about whether they have made the right choice, because they know how to analyze the risks and plan properly. And they understand the importance of time management. The knowledge of time management enables them to meet deadlines. This gives them a feeling of accomplishment, which boosts their confidence. They feel energized, which motivates them to achieve more in life.

Time management and willpower go hand in hand. In order to apply your time management skill, you'll need to apply your willpower. Willpower is needed to tune out the distractions and stick to your plan in an effective manner. Therefore if you have the knowledge of time management, and you don't use your willpower, that knowledge is useless. Today we will learn how to become excellent at time management using our willpower.

Working Smarter, Not harder

Everyone can be busy, but not everyone is good at time management. If you're good at time management, you'll still be busy, but you'll also be more productive. Learning to manage times enables you to accomplish more tasks in shorter period of time, which leads to more free time. This helps you to stay focused, which leads to more success in professional life. Time manage is critical for personal life and career success.

By learning time management you can organize your day so that you can make the use of every moment. Knowing how to mage your time means, you'll work smarter with less effort. By learning to use time wisely, you can obtain more free time— and if you get an extra hour of productivity in 24 hours, you can gain an additional 250 productive hours at work every year.

So let's learn how to utilize our time. Here are some time management techniques:

* Make a to-do list in the morning on a paper or using a task management app or online project management tool, and list all the tasks you want to accomplish today. This may sound very simple, but you have to start somewhere.

Now look at the list and rank them in order of priority. Are there some tasks that are urgent and must be completed by day's end? Are there others that need to be completed by the end of this week? Rank the tasks according to importance and urgency, then start with the task that is most urgent.

* Delegating is a good way to ensure that more works get accomplished in less time. The flip side of delegating is taking all the tasks on your shoulders. If you have an option of sharing the workload, you should utilize it. Delegating frees you up to tackle the most important aspects of your project. In workplace delegating not just saves time, it increases the confidence and productivity of your subordinates. If you give important responsibilities to your employees along with the freedom of doing their works their way, it will build your employees' skill, innovation along with your company's productivity. If you don't delegate in your workplace, you're sending a strong signal to your subordinates that you don't believe they have skills and experience for doing the tasks they were hired for. By transferring some of your

responsibilities, you can be more efficient and productive at tasks that are most important.

* Don't strive for perfection. Perfectionism is about paying too much attention to every detail regardless of their importance, and this is a kind of procrastination. Remember there is noting wrong with being ordinary. You don't always have to be perfect. A perfectionist often sets unattainable expectations of themselves, and adds stress to their life.

* Multitasking saves time, although some multitasking is dangerous. For instance, if you drive while talking on the phone, there is a chance of accident. But there are many tasks you can combine safely and do effectively. This will save a good amount of time. However you'll need some practice for doing more than one work at the same time. Make sure multitask does not overwhelm you and create unnecessary stress.

* Learn to slow down. Slowing down and de-stressing is important to maintain your highest level of mental functioning.

* Turn off social media app alert. This is a big time waster. You don't need moment-to-moment update on everything happening with your friends.

* De-clutter and organize. Follow the de- cluttering techniques discussed in chapter one. Clutter in your environment can distract you. Therefore make sure everything is organized in your workplace.

Time is a finite resource. No matter how you slice it, you only have 24 hours in a day. You can't add an extra hour. If you lose money, you might get it back, but if an hour is wasted, it will not come back at any cost. Time is the most precious thing. Therefore make the best use of your time.

"IN ANY MOMENT OF DECISION, THE BEST THING YOU CAN DO IS THE RIGHT THING, THE NEXT BEST THING IS THE WRONG THING, AND THE WORST THING YOU CAN DO IS NOTHING."

- THEODORE ROOSEVELT

DAY SEVENTEEN

Choice overload and Willpower Depletion

It takes lots of mental effort to make a decision. Making choices reduces our mental energy, persistence and willpower. If we allow ourselves making too many decisions in a day, our willpower will get exhausted to the point where we end up making increasingly poor, even self-destructive decisions. This condition is called "decision fatigue".

We already know that willpower is like a muscle, and it gets fatigued when we keep using it over and over again.

Making a decision is like doing another rap in the gym and when we take too many decisions, the strength of our willpower muscle diminishes and we experience decision fatigue. Every one of us experiences this condition when they spend a decision-heavy day at work. When our willpower muscle gets overloaded, we have to take a break and avoid making decisions.

Remember mental energy is precious, so we have to be careful about not wasting it. If we overwhelm ourselves with too many decisions, we are likely to make mistakes, which could delay our progress and destroy our motivation. Therefore we have to put limits over our choices and make the best decision.

Today we will learn how to eliminate unnecessary decisions and protect ourselves from decision fatigue.

Avoiding Decision Fatigue

To ensure that you don't unwittingly let reduced willpower derail your hard work, you have to learn how to limit the amount of decisions you make throughout the day. Here are the ways to overcome decision fatigue:

- Plan in advance. You can plan some of the daily decisions the night before. Small decisions like what should you eat for breakfast tomorrow or whether you should go to the dry cleaner before or after work, can be taken the night before. These kinds of decisions may take only few minutes, but it will give you more mental space to make important decisions on the next day.

- This may sound obvious, but the best time to make an important decision is when you start your day. A study involving medical decisions revealed that clinicians were more likely to prescribe unnecessary antibiotics for acute respiratory infections (ARIs) as clinic sessions wore on. The researchers hypothesized that the mental work of evaluating patient after patient progressively impaired their ability to resist making potentially inappropriate choices. When we are well rested and fully energized, our brain functions optimally and we can make hard decisions with ease. As the day progresses our willpower and self-control depletes. The early morning decisions, choices that are made after meals are best because they are based on emotion and intuition as well as logic. Therefore make your important decisions in the morning.

- When we experience decision fatigue, we feel out of control. And one of the quickest ways to regain the sense of control is to build a momentum around tasks. Chain similar tasks together. This will reduce the stress of decision-making and will cause you to feel the niggling urge to continue your work until you finish it. This psychological phenomenon is called Zeigarnik effect.

When you schedule similar tasks together, your mind will perceive it as a single task. As you start working with one task, the mind will build a momentum to complete all the tasks in the chain. You may take a break for a day, but your subconscious mind will keep working on it. That's why novelist Ernest Hemingway used to finish his writing in the mid sentence. Build your own momentum either by chaining the similar tasks together or following Hemingway's example.

- Put limits on your choices. Choices certainly give us the autonomy and the opportunity to pursue our intentions and desires. But having too many choices can be demotivating. Because when we think about lots of choices, we experience choice overload. Too many choices lead us down the road of indecision and to paralysis by analysis; as a result we may end up with making no choice. To avoid this situation, we have to deliberately limit our choice.

The trick to limit the choice is to figure out what things you're willing to accept and what things you are unwilling to compromise on. Once you do that, gently narrow the options to pursue.

Start with limiting choices in one area of your life for a week. This could be the foods you eat, the TV programs you watch, the blogs you read or the things you do in weekend. Whatever it is, intentionally limit your choice in that area for the next seven days.

After you're done keeping a handful of choices, you've to consciously block everything else out.

97

This may require some degree of self-discipline, but it's an important part of the experiment.

Then fully commit to your choice.

"THE LESS YOU RESPOND TO NEGATIVE PEOPLE,

THE MORE PEACEFUL YOUR LIFE WILL BECOME."

– BRYCE LEWIS

DAY EIGHTEEN

People Who Drain You

The old adage of quality over quantity still holds values in today's world— not just in business but also in relationships. In this modern age of social media people just keep on growing their network, even if some of the people in their lives already suck the life out of them. But it is important to protect ourselves from negative people. With their bad attitudes, catastrophic thinking and fatalistic outlooks, they can ruin your confidence and willpower. They will not just discourage you to take challenges, but drag you down with them to the dark side.

Do you know people who constantly complain about their lives? They may have legitimate problems, but they seem to enjoy wallowing in their misery instead of trying to work their way through obstacles? They can be your acquaintances, friends, neighbors or co-workers. You have to choose not to listen to those people.

While positive people can boost your mood and raise your vibration, negative people do the opposite— they tend to be an energy drain. They will suck the positive energy out of you to fuel their negativity and leave you emotionally drained and depressed.

Many times we unwittingly give those negative individuals influence over our thoughts, behaviors and feelings. These people are great at discouraging and giving you negative feedback. If you hang around with them enough, and listen to them long enough, you'll start to feel that you're having negative self-talks. So what we can do to weed out these negative people? In this session we will learn about that.

Weeding Out the Negative Influences

It is not easy to get rid of negative people, because sometimes they are inextricably bound up with our work or family lives. Most people cling to negative individuals because of a feeling of loyalty. Negative people also clings on, and they can make you feel guilty if you try to remove them form your life. In order to cut these people out of your life, first we have to identify them. Here are some of the classic signs of negative people:

- They will try to control you either through overt methods or subtle manipulation. This may sound strange, these people have no control over their lives, but the always tend to control the life of others.

- These people don't respect other's boundaries. If you're always asking someone not to behave toward you in a particular way, and they don't care, that person is probably toxic. A well-adjusted individual always respects other's boundaries. But negative people thrive on violating them.

- These people are there to take what they can get from you, but they hardly show any signs of giving

101

something back. Although it needn't has to be equal, healthy give and take is crucial for sustaining a friendship.

- These people are usually dishonest and selfish.
- They always look for ways to feel oppressed. They tend to play victim card to make others feel guilty
- They rarely admit their fault. They always try to find ways to be right, even when they are not.
- They always try to avoid responsibility.

Removing these people from your life can blow up in your face. But that's part of the process. So how do you go about getting rid of these people? Here are some suggestions:

- Start with social media, such as Facebook. There are surely many people on your newsfeed whose updates you don't want to see, and yet you feel like you're forced to deal with them. Either un-follow or un-friend those people. You're actually not obliged to be their friends your whole life.
- Don't be too nice with those people. This may sound hash, but this kind of people tends to take

advantage of any kindness that's imparted on them.

- If you can't detach them completely, limit the amount of time you spend with these people. Don't feel like you own them a huge explanation if they fail to keep in touch with you.

- These people are great at showing up when they need something, particularly when they are in trouble. You don't have to always solve their problems. It's not your responsibility.

- Don't argue with these people. It's tempting to fall into the dynamic of negativity by arguing— that is what these people do. Firmly restate your boundaries. Giving up the argument may refrain them from bothering you.

"A BIG PART OF WILLPOWER IS HAVING SOMETHING TO ASPIRE TO, SOMETHING TO LIVE FOR." - MARK SHUTTLEWORTH

DAY NINETEEN

Motivation: The Fuel of Willpower

One of the biggest challenges in reaching any goal is finding motivation to stick to it. If you don't feel motivated, you are likely to quit. But if you manage to stick with a goal for long enough, you'll reach there eventually. Achieving a goal takes determination, patience and motivation. It is motivation that empowers your willpower and drives you towards your goal. Motivation keeps you going when things get tough. It makes you to work harder under tremendous pressure, and accomplish the task. Motivation is the force that pushes you to give one more try when all the conditions are conducive for you to give up. Motivation is the fuel of your willpower, and without motivation, working on your goal is like driving a car without fuel. Today we will discuss about how to find motivation.

Finding Motivation

Motivation is crucial for success, but finding it may not always be easy. Failure is easy, because to fail in something, you don't need any action on your part, it just happens. But motivation requires action. Many people start with huge motivation, but when they face difficulties, their motivation drops. Motivation also disappears when you're not doing what you love. It is hard to motivate yourself to do something you really don't want to do or something you really don't like to do. But if you motivate yourself to do something you love, you can sustain your effort for long enough until it turns into your passion. Here are some effective tips for staying motivated:

- Always start small. If you start out big, you may lose motivation quite easily. Start with a ridiculously small step; then grow from there. For instance, if you want to incorporate workouts into your daily routine, don't start with intense workouts. Instead start with some easy warm up exercises for five minutes everyday. You may want to do more, but commit to five minutes for one week. It's very easy; you can't fail. If you are successful, increase it to 10 minutes for next one week. In a month, you'll be doing 30-45 minutes. Baby steps may seem insignificant when you look at the big picture, but it quickly adds up.

- It's better not to start with many goals at a time. Working on multiple goals at once can make you feel overwhelmed, and sap your energy and motivation. It's a common mistake many of us make. You can't maintain energy and focus if you attempt to achieve two major goals at the same time. Therefore pick one goal, and pay your complete attention on that goal. Once the goal is achieved, you'll feel a sense of accomplishment, and mental energy to meet the next goal.

- Excuses can be our friend, but can also be our big enemy. Look your excuses in the eye and ask yourself, is it that hard to move on? The negative forces in the mind will try to hold you back. If you find yourself using an excuse for postponing your work for later, use this technique. Don't believe your own baloney reasons, find out if the mind is tricking you.

- One of the effective ways to stay motivated is to stay accountable. You can commit to yourself to a group of people through online groups (i.e. such as Facebook groups) or blogs and choose to stay accountable to that forum. Commit to report to that group of people once a week and stick to it. This will motivate you to do better, because you won't like to report that you've failed.

- Listen to motivational speeches. It will give you a quick boost of inspiration. There are hundreds of motivational videos in YouTube. Also watch acceptance speeches. Because watching someone at their best will make you feel exited and inspire you to succeed.

"REVIEW YOUR GOALS TWICE EVERY DAY IN
ORDER TO BE FOCUSED ON ACHIEVING THEM."

- LES BROWN

DAY TWENTY

When To Review Progress

Periodically, you have to check with the progress on the goal you've set because there is a little point of having a goal if you never know whether you are making any progress. Therefore measure and review your progress regularly.

You can review your progress once in a day, in a week or month. Daily is too frequent as unexpected things happen all the time. Monthly is too infrequent because you need to make adjustment before too much time has lapsed. I recommend that you review your progress once a week. So let us learn how to review our progress.

Measuring and Evaluating Your Progress

Measuring your progress is important, because if you don't track your progress, you won't know if you are moving in the right direction. Looking at the record of your progress, you can see how you're coming along. Monitoring and evaluating your progress makes it easier to identify what you need to address next. There are different methods for measuring progress. Some of the methods may not be available to you. Depending on the type of goal you have to choose the right measuring tool.

Quantitative measurement is far simpler and more specific than qualitative. Look if you can find a way to quantify the progress of the goal you've set. Although you can't quantify the progress of all goals, in the cases of vast majority of goals, you can. Sometimes there is more than one way to quantify your progress. For instance, if your goal is to lose weight, you can use a weighting scale to measure the weight lost or a measuring tap to measure the inches lost. You can also use body fat calipers to measure the changes of your body fat percentage.

Maintain a record of your progress as you move along, accompanied by some personal notes. When a problem arise or if you fail to meet a target, these notes will give you some clue and help you to understand what went wrong and how you can fix it. You'll be able to see what works and what does not work.

We have discussed that you have to break down a big goal into small steps. If you've done that, you must have a list of tasks, which need to be completed, and a deadline for each task. Create a checklist out of this list and once you complete a task, simply tick it off and make note of the date of completion. Review your progress regularly, and when you do, use this checklist to find out if any corrective action needs to be taken.

Not all progresses can be measured using quantitative methods. There are also goals, which are qualitative in nature, e.g. being a good public speaker, or improving self-esteem. If your goal is qualitative in nature, you can still track your progress.

Develop a rating system to monitor the process. Rank your progress using a scale of $1 - 10$, with 10 being the highest and 1 being lowest level of progress.

As you measure your progress on a regular basis, you'll experience an increased motivation and willpower when you realize that day-by-day you are stepping closer to your goal. In order to make an effective decision, you've to know where you stand. You can know that if you measure your progress and maintain a record.

Answer the following questions once you're done reviewing your goal:

1. Are you still on the track to attaining your goal?

2. Is there anything that is holding you back?

3. Is the goal is harder or easier than expected?

4. Do you think you need smaller steps?

5. Overall how satisfied you are with the progress? If you're not satisfied, find out what slowing you down and fix the problem.

6. Is there anything you need to do better?

7. Are you enjoying this process of moving closer toward your goal?

"AFFIRMATIONS ARE OUR MENTAL VITAMINS,

PROVIDING THE SUPPLEMENTARY POSITIVE

THOUGHTS WE NEED TO BALANCE THE BARRAGE

OF NEGATIVE EVENTS AND THOUGHTS WE

EXPERIENCE DAILY."

- TIA WALKER

DAY TWENTY ONE

Affirmations for Rock Solid Willpower

Affirmations are the positive statements that you consciously choose to either help removing something from your life, or help adding something new in your life. These are the mantras to keep you in constant positive mood, and help you to become who you want to be. These mantras can purify your thoughts and restructure the dynamic of your brain so that you truly begin to see the positive in every aspect of your life. Positive affirmations will elevate your willpower, and motivate you to push through when the going gets tough.

Today is the last day of our willpower challenge. Use the willpower strategies you've learned in this book to transform your life and use the following affirmations to boost your willpower.

Boosting willpower with Power Affirmations

Positive affirmations can be practiced anytime. But the best time is in the morning. You can use a mirror and look yourself in the eye while repeating the following statements. Take a moment to relax and clear your mind. When you are ready gently say the affirmations to yourself:

- I am in complete control over myself
- I can control my desires
- I'm superior to negative thoughts and low actions
- I take responsibility for my own actions
- I always keep on going no matter how hard things get
- I possess all the qualities to be successful
- My ability to conquer challenges is limitless

- I'm persistent in pursuing my goal.
- I have the willpower to remove all my bad habits
- I'm above all the distractions and temptations
- I acknowledge my self worth; my confidence is soaring
- I'm completely in charge of my life
- My willpower is getting stronger everyday
- I'm the architect of my life
- I design my destiny
- My life is just beginning
- I'm a powerhouse
- All is well in my life
- I can easily tap into my willpower
- The challenges I face, give me energy and purpose
- I love hard work. It energizes me and brings me focus
- My success is inevitable if I keep working hard to reach my goals
- I'm determined in achieving my goals

"THE TIME FOR ACTION IS NOW. IT'S NEVER TOO LATE TO DO SOMETHING."

- CARL SANDBURG

CLOSING COMMENTS

In the last twenty days you've learned how to make the best use of your willpower to reach any goal. You've learned how to apply the willpower strategies to solve problems, remove obstacles, develop positive habits, build emotional resilience and empower the vision. You've also learned how to train your willpower, strengthen your willpower and conserve your willpower. The lessons you've learned in this book will help you to stay inspired and focused in tough times, and achieve success against the odds.

www.ingramcontent.com/pod-product-compliance
Lightning Source LLC
Chambersburg PA
CBHW071322220526
45468CB00001B/461